DOMINIC
THE DINOSAUR
ADVENTURER

By: Tiffany Thomas & Dominic Swaby

This Book Belongs To:

_____

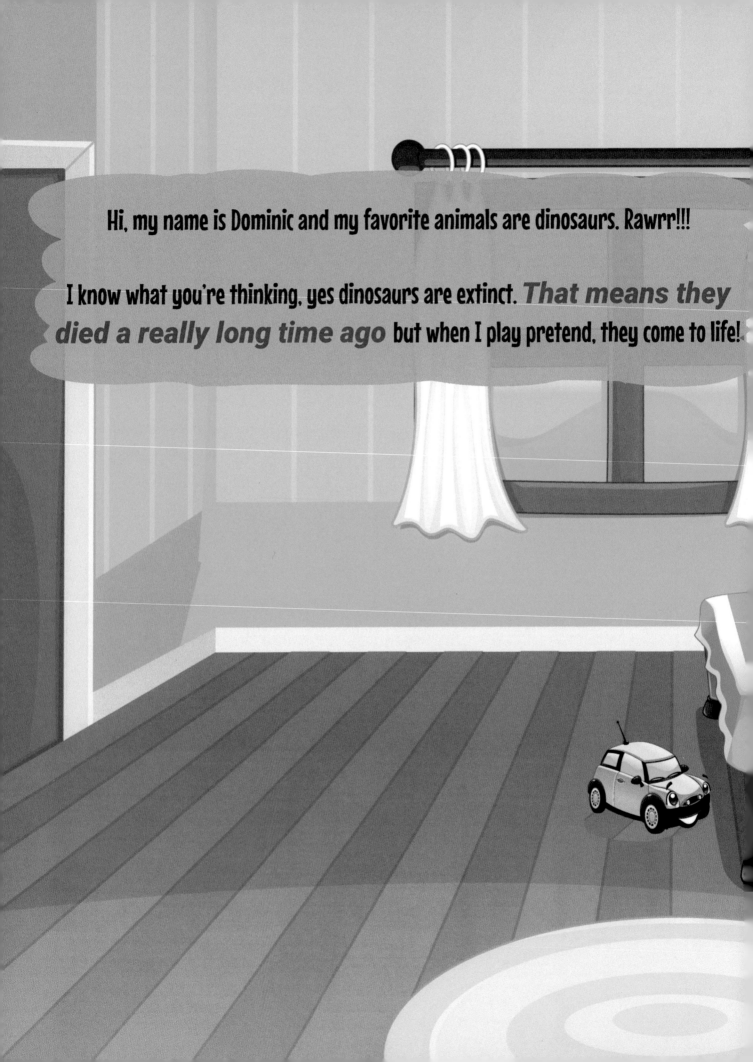

Hi, my name is Dominic and my favorite animals are dinosaurs. Rawrr!!!

I know what you're thinking, yes dinosaurs are extinct. *That means they died a really long time ago* but when I play pretend, they come to life!

I like to dress up as a famous paleontologist, *that's someone who studies dinosaurs* and talk about the different dinosaurs that lived millions of years ago. It's a lot of fun, would you like to come along?

Great! Time to go on a dinosaur adventure, let's travel back in time. I will introduce you to all my dinosaur friends. You'll need a grown-up to help with some of these words but don't worry, it's easy once you get a hang of it.

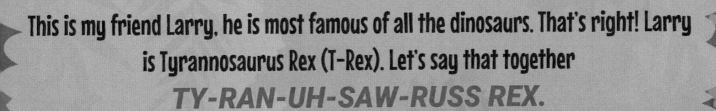

This is my friend Larry, he is most famous of all the dinosaurs. That's right! Larry is Tyrannosaurus Rex (T-Rex). Let's say that together
TY-RAN-UH-SAW-RUSS REX.

Good Job! Larry is really big and quick; he weighs as much as four rhinos. That's huge! Stomping through the forest. Larry can move about 12 miles per hour. He walks on two legs and uses his large head to balance his long tail. Larry is a carnivore, that means he likes to eat meat. He can see and smell very well: this makes it easy for him to find a meal-that's if his loud roar doesn't scare them off first.

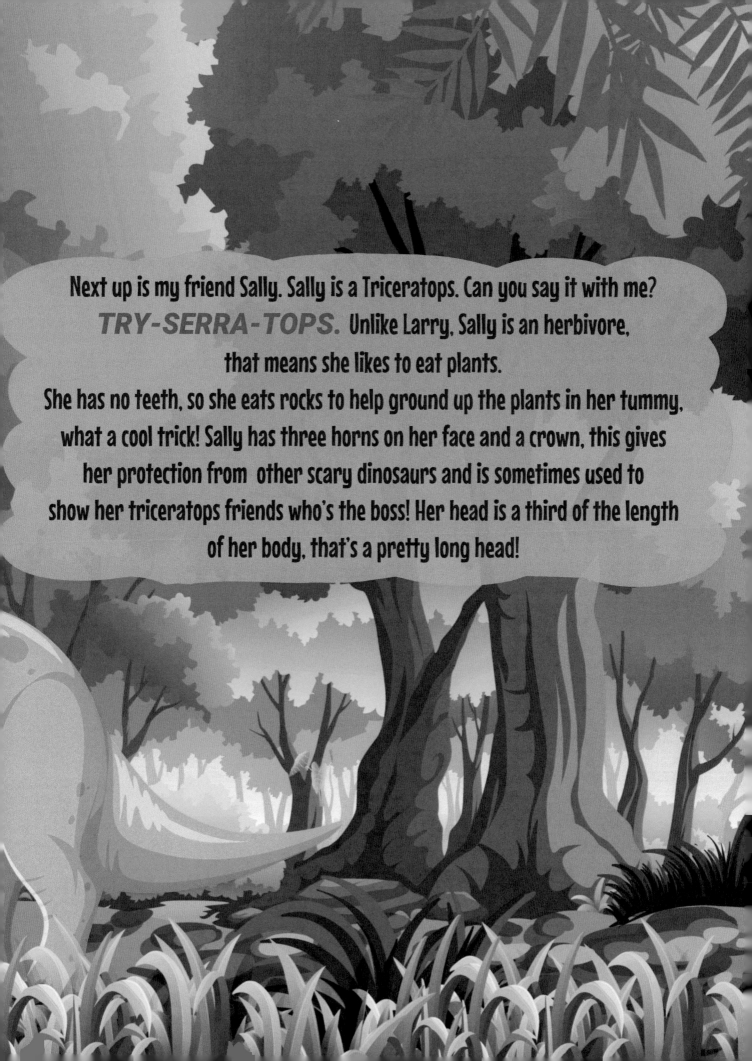

Next up is my friend Sally. Sally is a Triceratops. Can you say it with me?
TRY-SERRA-TOPS. Unlike Larry, Sally is an herbivore,
that means she likes to eat plants.
She has no teeth, so she eats rocks to help ground up the plants in her tummy,
what a cool trick! Sally has three horns on her face and a crown, this gives
her protection from other scary dinosaurs and is sometimes used to
show her triceratops friends who's the boss! Her head is a third of the length
of her body, that's a pretty long head!

Meet my friend Henry, he is an Allosaurus. Say *A-LUH-SAW-RUHS*. Henry is a carnivore like Larry the T Rex. He has a lot of teeth but they are all curved backwards, so when he holds on to his dinner, it has no chance of getting away. Henry has a large skull and walks on two legs.

He can run an impressive 21 miles an hour, that's almost as fast as a car driving through a neighborhood. Allosaurus dinosaurs like to hunt large animals even the giant plant-eating dinosaur Apatosaurus, Allosaurus bite mark was even found on the neck plate of a Stegosaurus! Hikes!

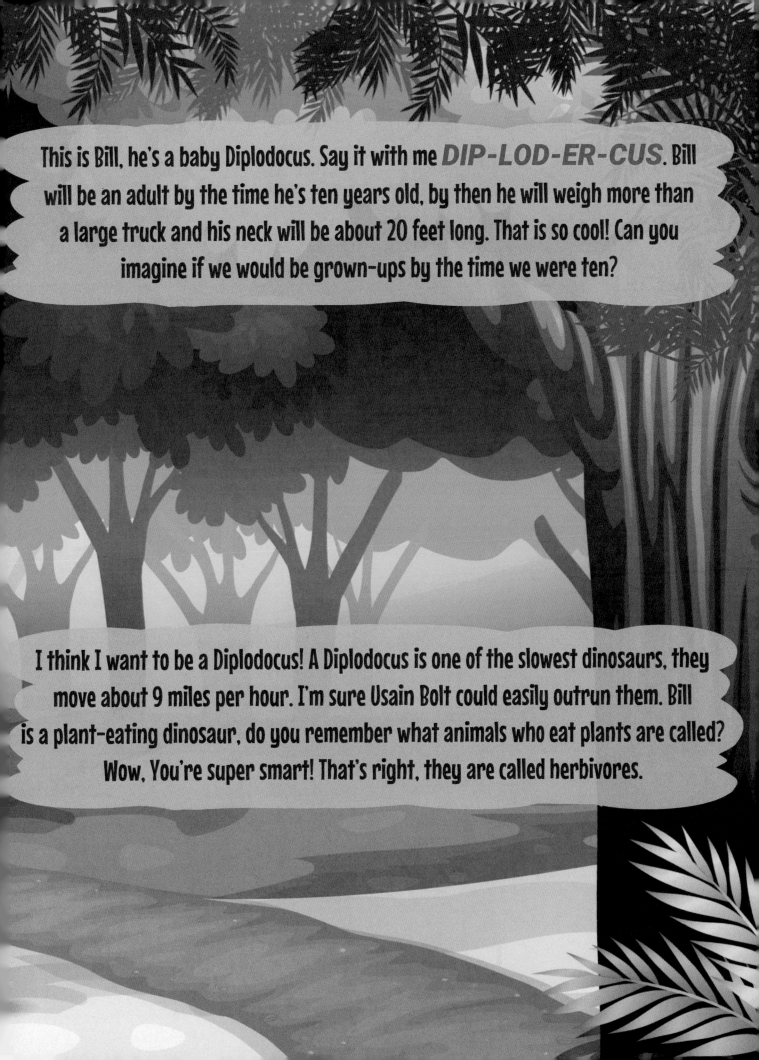

This is Bill, he's a baby Diplodocus. Say it with me **DIP-LOD-ER-CUS**. Bill will be an adult by the time he's ten years old, by then he will weigh more than a large truck and his neck will be about 20 feet long. That is so cool! Can you imagine if we would be grown-ups by the time we were ten?

I think I want to be a Diplodocus! A Diplodocus is one of the slowest dinosaurs, they move about 9 miles per hour. I'm sure Usain Bolt could easily outrun them. Bill is a plant-eating dinosaur, do you remember what animals who eat plants are called? Wow, You're super smart! That's right, they are called herbivores.

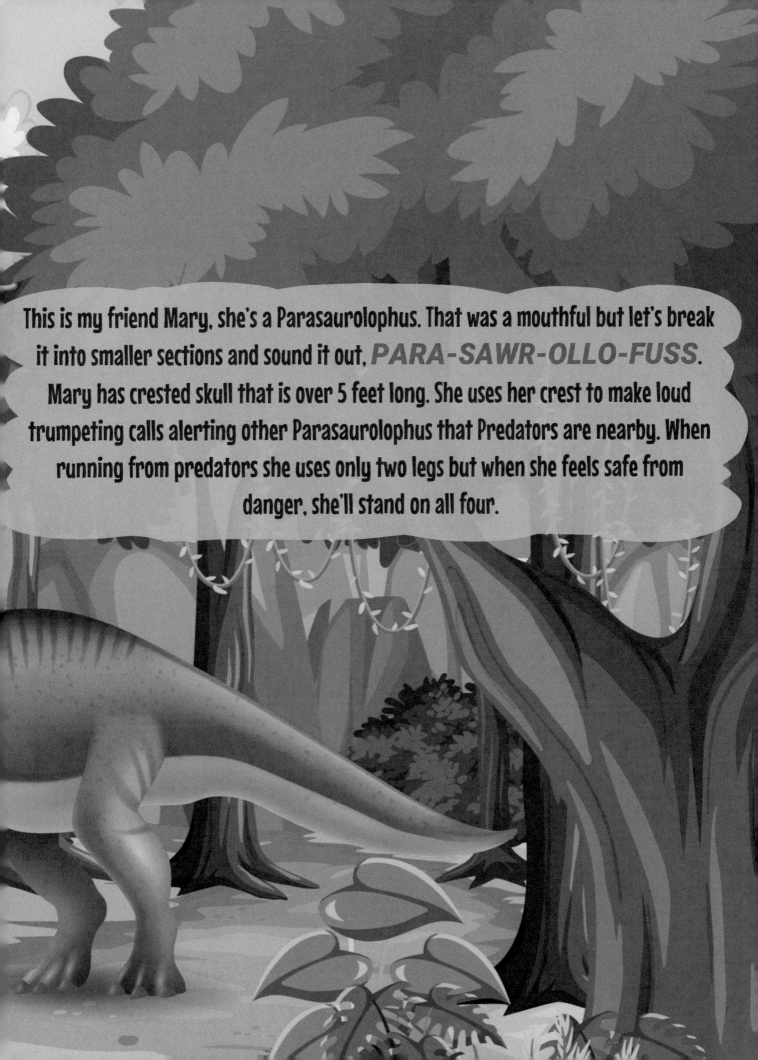

This is my friend Mary, she's a Parasaurolophus. That was a mouthful but let's break it into smaller sections and sound it out, *PARA-SAWR-OLLO-FUSS*. Mary has crested skull that is over 5 feet long. She uses her crest to make loud trumpeting calls alerting other Parasaurolophus that Predators are nearby. When running from predators she uses only two legs but when she feels safe from danger, she'll stand on all four.

This is my good pal Mike, he's an Ankylosaurus. Let's say it together **AN-KEE-LO-SAUR-URS**. Mike looks like a crocodile but he's a herbivore, he likes to eat ferns that line the shore of the water. Mike is as big as an army tank and his powerful tail is strong enough to break the bones of his predators. I wouldn't want to mess with Mike!

My friend Louis is a Velociraptor. Say it slowly **VEL-LOH-SIH-RAP-TUH**, sometimes they are just called raptors. Louis is a carnivore and hunts in a pack of other Velociraptors to take down large plant-eating dinosaurs.

That is pretty impressive for his size, he is about the size of a turkey. Louis and his friends can run 24 miles an hour and they are pretty good at stealing meals from other dinosaurs. That is how they got their name, Velociraptor means swift thief. I think it's safe to say Velociraptors are pretty naughty but they are one of the smartest dinosaurs.

Old lady Jones may be slow but she is strong, she is a Stegosaurus. Let's say that again **STEG-GO-SAW-RUSS**. Old lady Jones has two rows of kite-shaped plates that stick out from her neck, back, and tail. She is as big as a bus but her brain is as small as a walnut, that means she wasn't as smart as other dinosaurs. Her plates and her three feet long spiked tail protect her from scary dinosaurs. Old lady Jones does not have a lot of teeth and she is a herbivore, she loves her yummy vegetables.

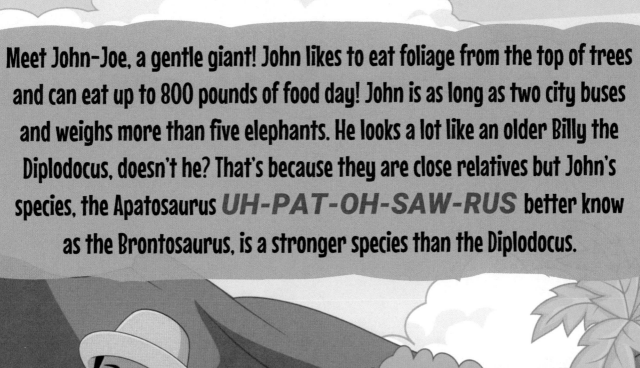

Meet John-Joe, a gentle giant! John likes to eat foliage from the top of trees and can eat up to 800 pounds of food day! John is as long as two city buses and weighs more than five elephants. He looks a lot like an older Billy the Diplodocus, doesn't he? That's because they are close relatives but John's species, the Apatosaurus **UH-PAT-OH-SAW-RUS** better know as the Brontosaurus, is a stronger species than the Diplodocus.

This dinosaur is one of the largest carnivores, and knows how to swim! That's right he is a Spinosaurus and his name is Jeff. Let's say it together *Spy-No-Saw-Russ*. Jeff weighs as much as three elephants and is as long as a semi-trailer truck! Spinosaurus means spine lizard because of the 7 feet long spines on its back. These Spines are longer than a human! Paleontologist like me believe that it is to keep him warm or attract other Spinosaurus. Jeff has large arms this means he can walk on two legs or all fours.

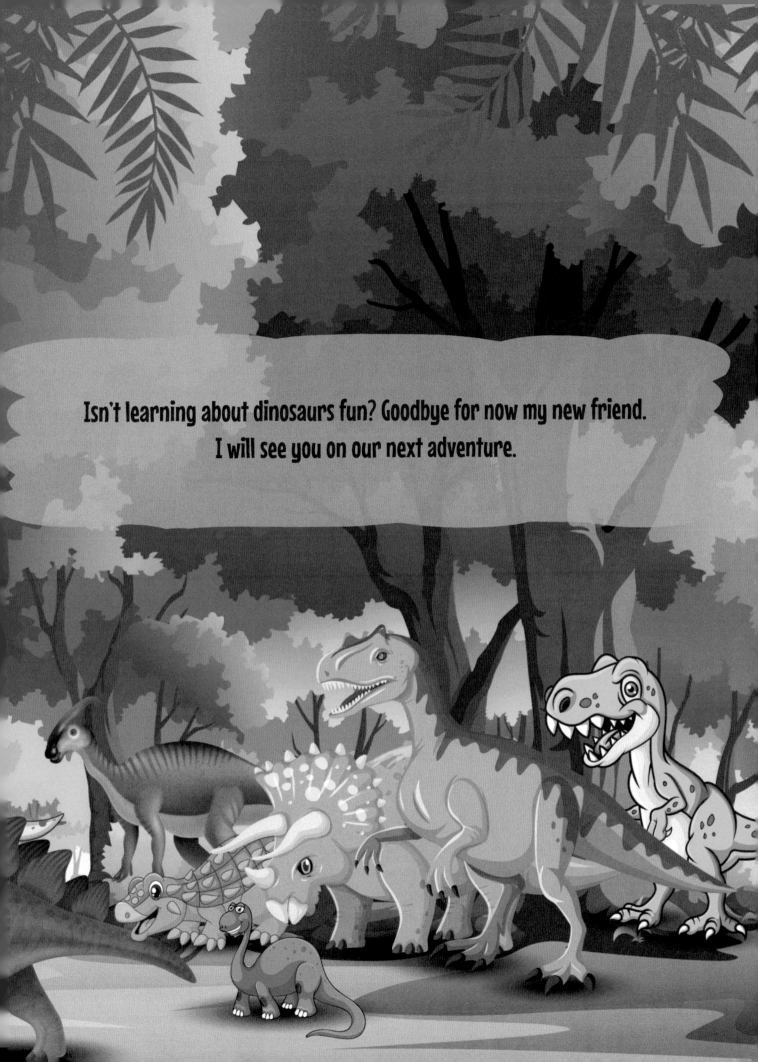

Isn't learning about dinosaurs fun? Goodbye for now my new friend.
I will see you on our next adventure.

Dedication

Happy Birthday
Dominic!

The End

Made in the USA
Middletown, DE
25 November 2023

43544230R00020